Drawing Cartoons from NUMBERS and LETTERS

125+ Step-by-Steps

Drawing Cartoons from NUMBERS and LETTERS

125+ Step-by-Steps

 Get Creative 6

Christopher Hart Books for KIDS

An imprint of Get Creative 6
19 West 21st Street, Suite 601
New York, NY 10010

Editor
PAMELA WISSMAN

Art Director
JOE VIOR

Production
J. ARTHUR MEDIA

Chief Executive Officer
CAROLINE KILMER

President
ART JOINNIDES

Chairman
JAY STEIN

What's Inside

Drawing is as Easy as 1 2 3, ABC!

Welcome, artists!

You can draw *zillions* of things by starting with a simple number or letter. With some clear instruction and a little imagination, you can draw a dinosaur by starting with the number 5, draw a robot starting with the letter A, and more. You'll see numbers and all the letters of the alphabet transform in front of your eyes into cartoon characters such as kings, cute girls, nerdy dads and more. It's like creating magic with a pencil. And you're the magician!

You can take any number or letter, and draw all kinds of characters. I've included enough simple steps so you can get the same amazing results you see here.

All you need to begin is a pencil. We'll start each character with a number or letter, and then add a few lines at each step. Once your drawing is the way you like it, you can add color, like I did, to make the cartoon stand out. You 'll soon be creating dozens of original cartoon characters. Let's get started!

Happy Drawing!
Christopher Hart

Numbers 1-9

If you can write the numbers 1 through 9, you can draw

anything! Get started by saying hello to these friendly

animals and characters.  It's the magic of cartooning.

All it takes is a pencil and your imagination.

Let the magic begin!

Absurd bird

Friendly frog

Duckling out for a swim

Friendly teen

Kid in a panic

A friend with feathers

Pterodactyl

The art of begging

Snail

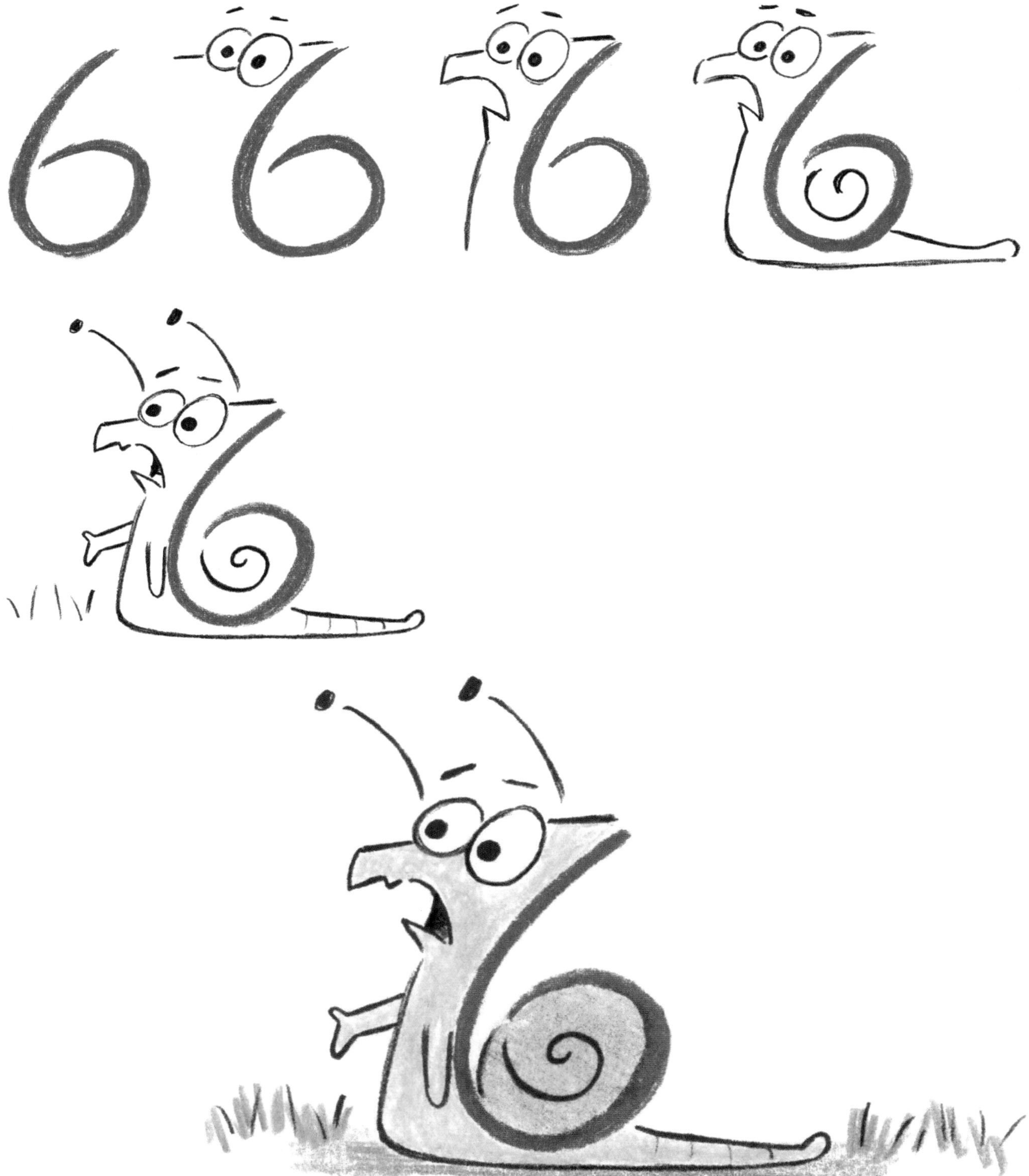

Chuckling bear

Pretty in pink

Bunny and egg

"You can never get a human on these things!"

Big nose bear

Basset hound

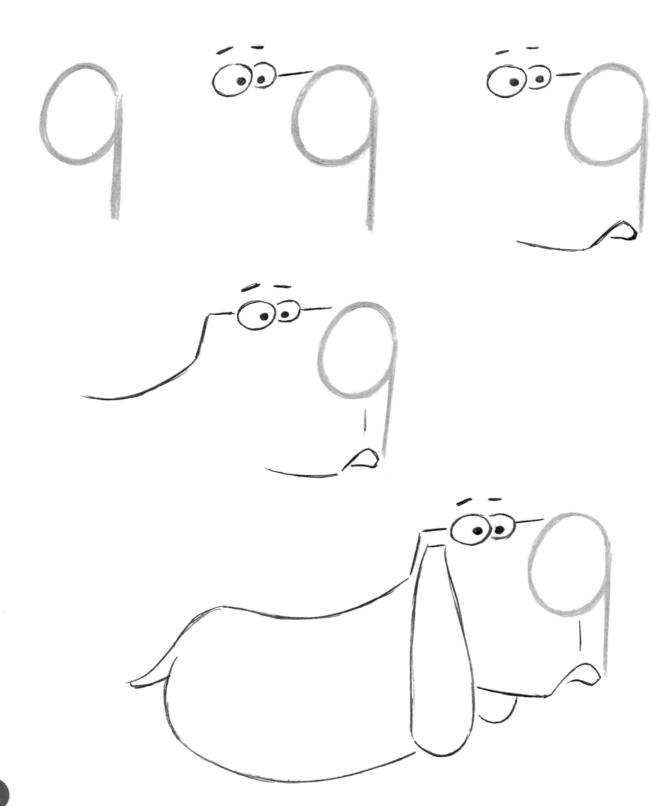

NuMBeRS 10-1001

WOOF!

Now let's make things a little more interesting by drawing

characters starting with two numbers. You'll learn how to

turn the number 10 into a simple  bird, transform the

number 20  into a little fish, and make an

imposing mean guy  from the number 30. Then

we'll begin to explore other numbers as examples of the funny

characters you can draw starting with just about any number

combination. There are no limits to what you can create!

Bird

Little Fish

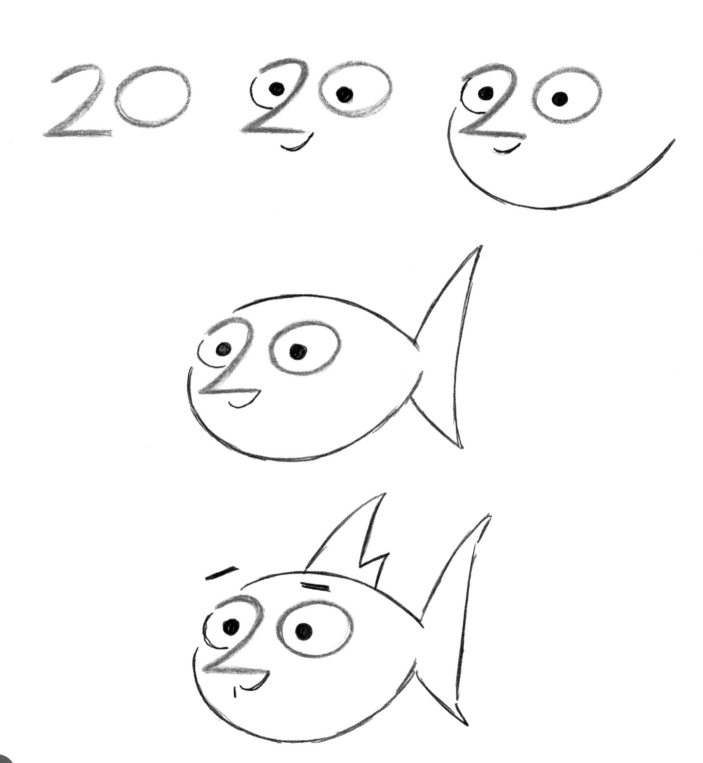

Mean guy

Good-mood monkey

Crocodile

Crabby

Mom and daughter kangaroo

Strolling elephant

Bunny with a snack

"What do you mean we're going extinct?"

53 5̊3 5̊3

Quirky glasses

WOOF!

Squeezable chipmunk

607

607

607

607

607

Raccoon

Letters A to Z

You've learned how to take simple numbers and turn them into cute animals, funny people, and other cartoony things.

Now, let's do the same thing with the letters of the alphabet!

Robot from galaxy X

Got it on sale

Defender of justice

Cool guy

B is for bee

Advisor to the queen

Funny dragon

En pointe

up to no good

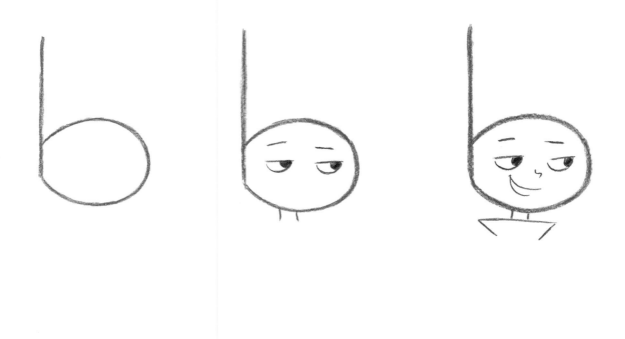

Shy girl

"Can you keep a secret?"

Psst—

Nervous knight

Dinosaur dash

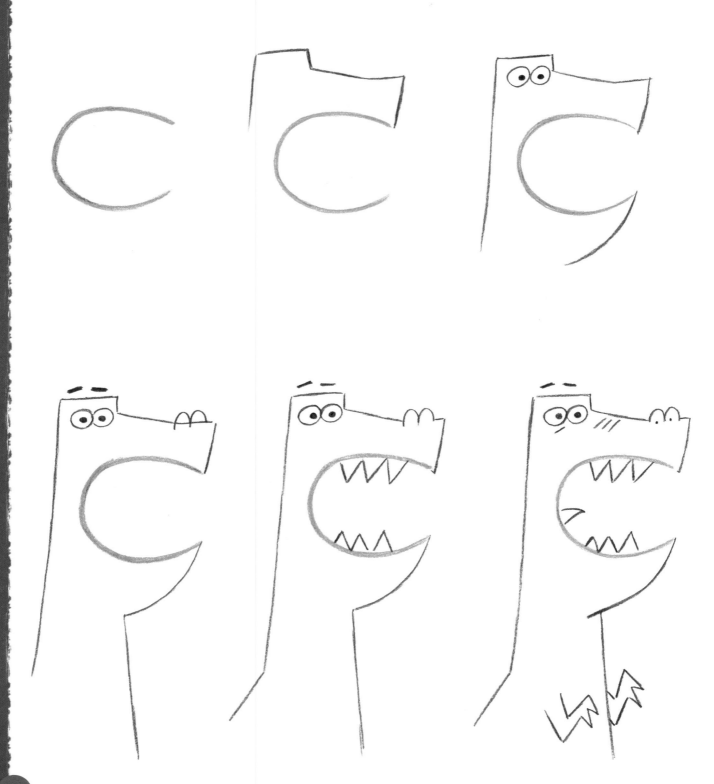

Grumpy Gary

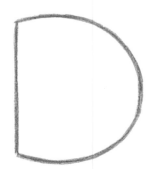

Little ladybug

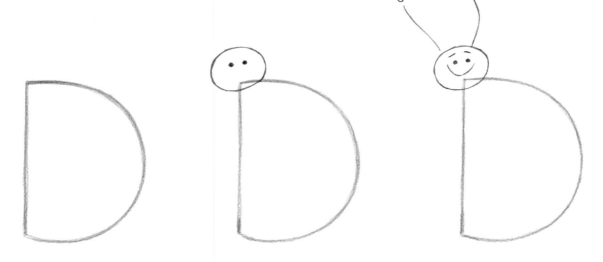

"I forgot my password"

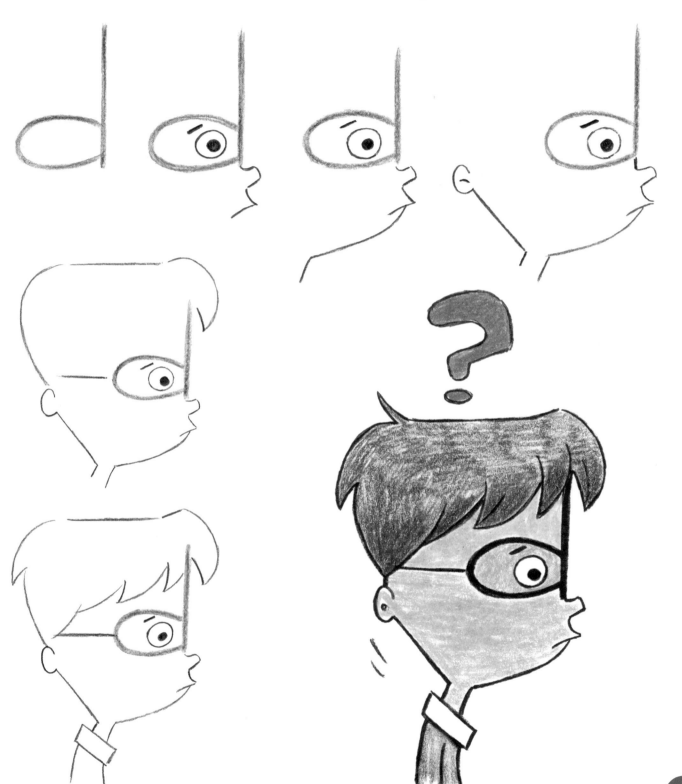

"Can I have a hug?"

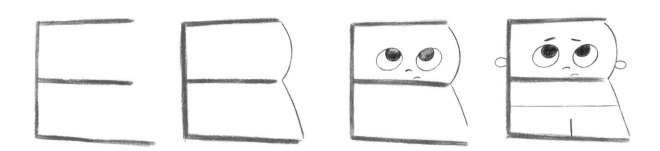

Little Leaguer

Scrubbed and ready

"Did I remember to lock the castle door?"

Stubborn Sam

Knowing smile

Summer hat

"For you, madame?"

In hot water

Super ponytail

Cool and casual

Know-it-all

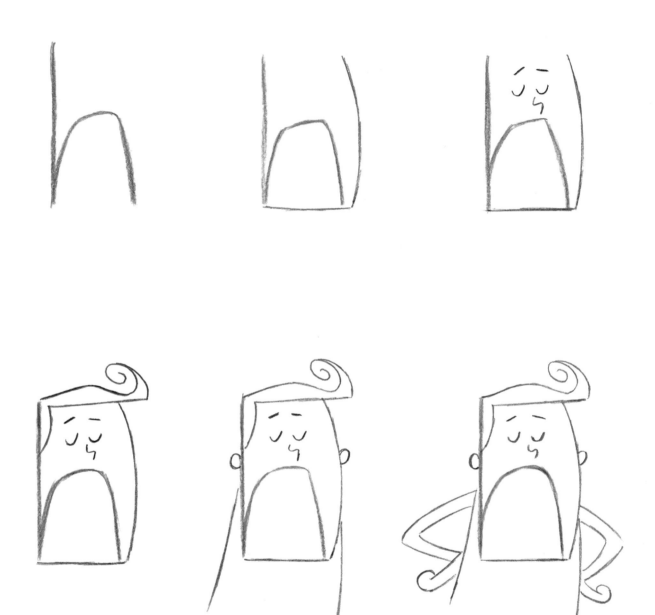

Spike

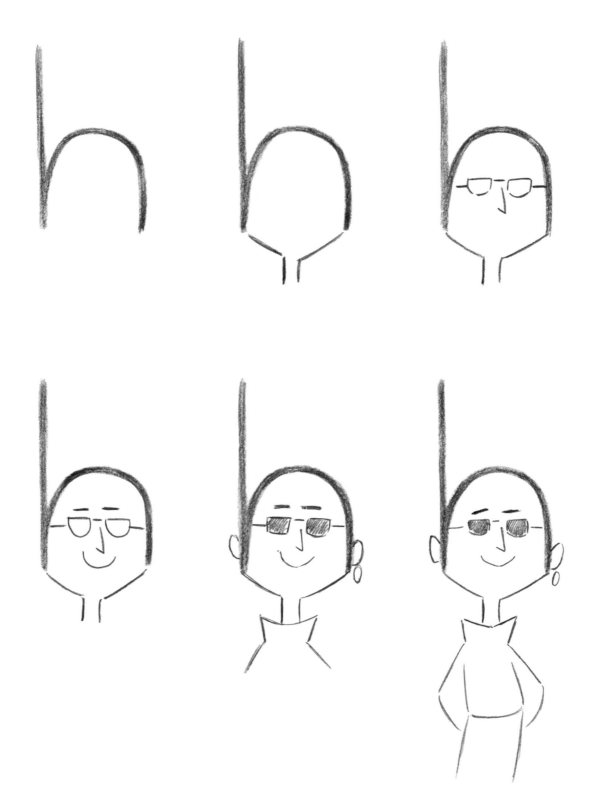

Amazing brainy head

The general

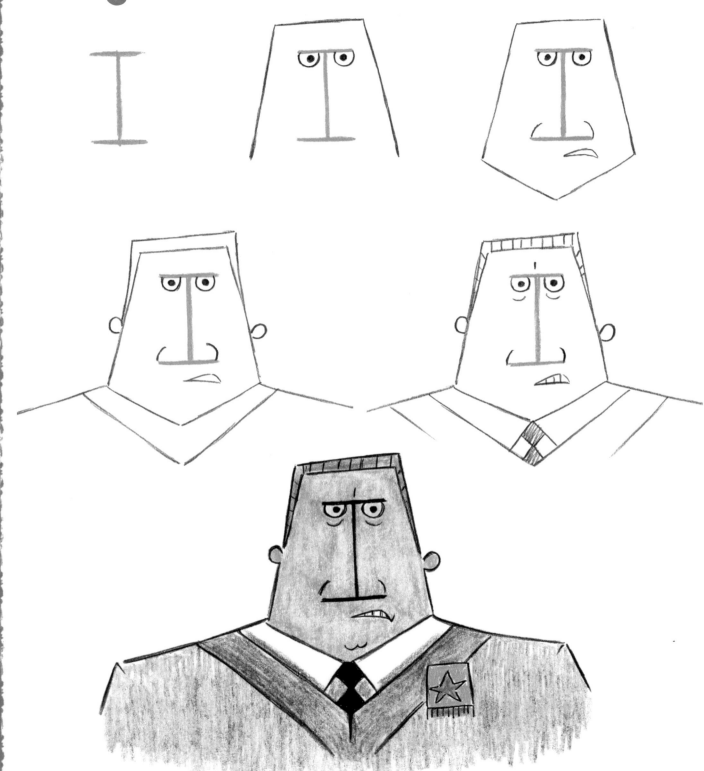

So trendy!

Taking the human for a walk

Surprised

J J J J J J J J J J

Sporty guy

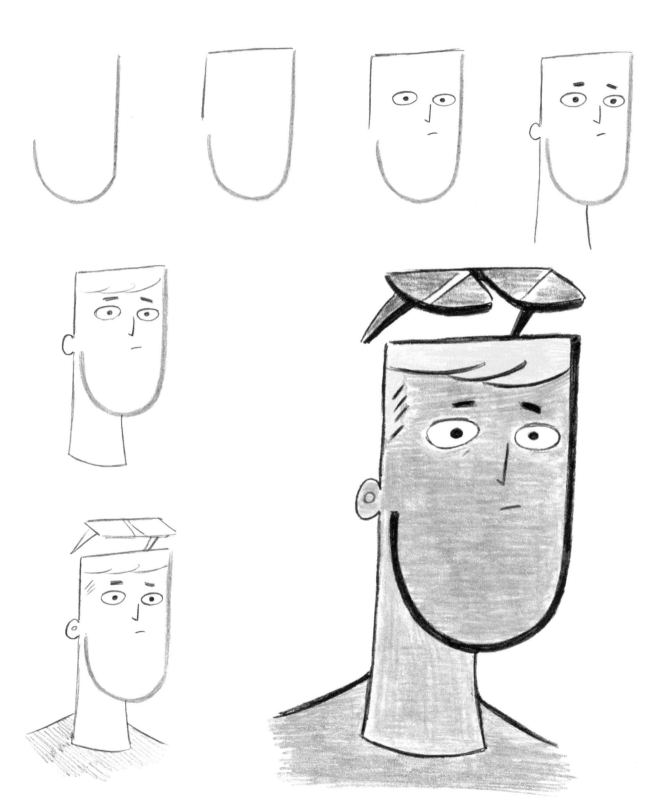

Secret service agent

Ready for bed!

Spooky and kooky

"you forgot someone!"

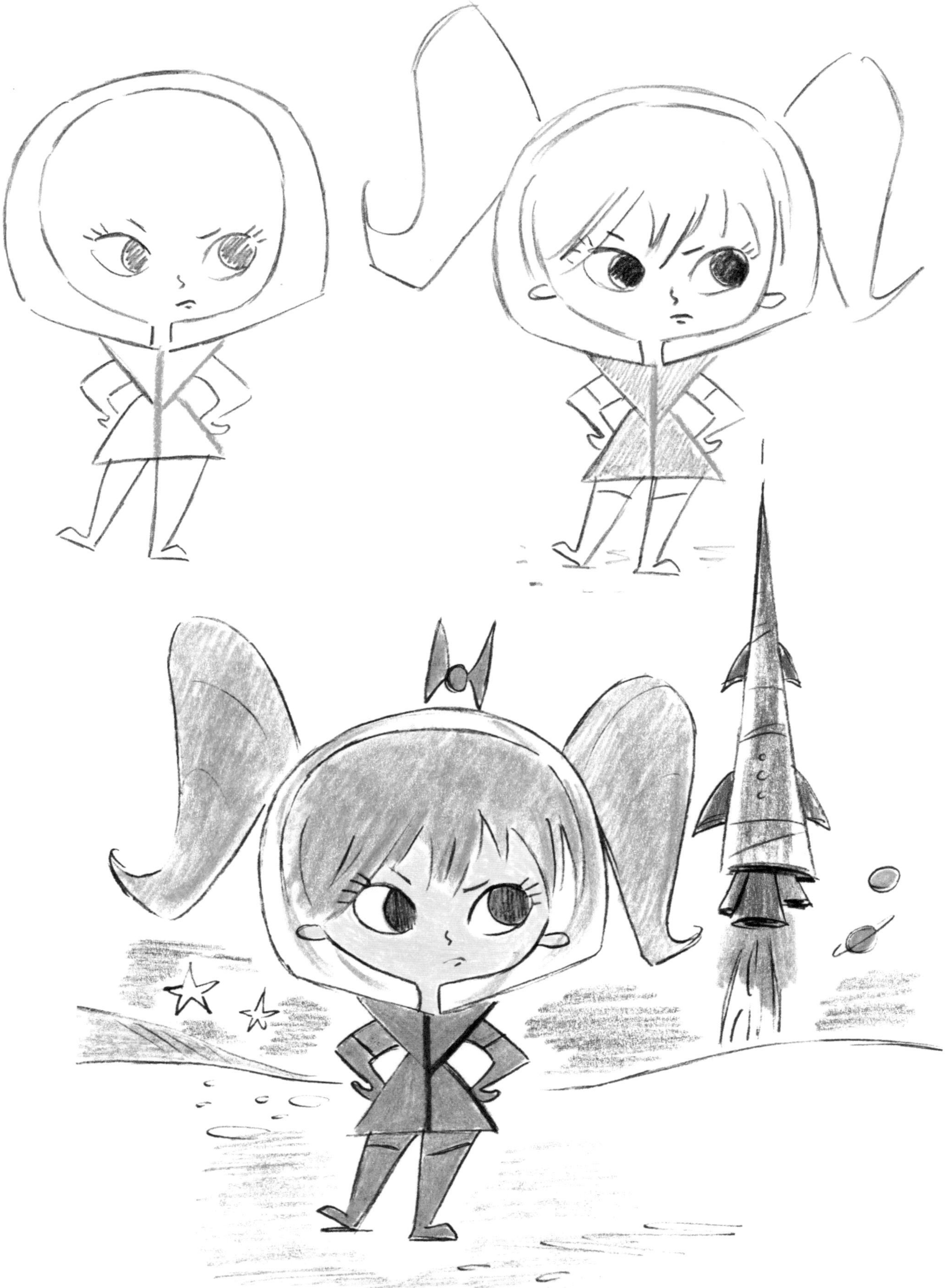

Shy smile

Zoom!

Goofy guy

"Eeeeek!"

Super spy

"Someday I'll be a cartoonist..."

"Happy Halloween!"

TRICK
OR
TREAT!

The latest hairstyle

Morning pick-me-up

Under the sea

  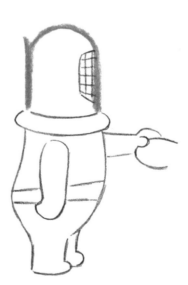

Pretty smile

Mystery man

Undercover agent

Cute and little

Got trees?

ultra chic

Mad scientist

Can burp the alphabet

Pretty in pink

The graduate

"See ya later!"

Secret mission

"Let's see... Where did I park?"

Funny kid

Opera singer

Big chin

"you're out!"

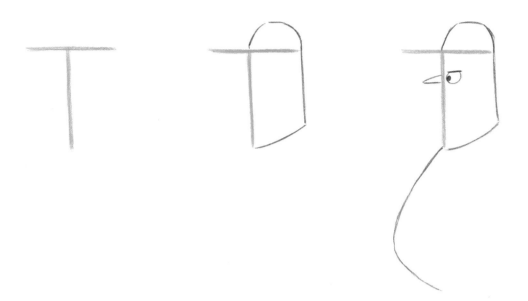

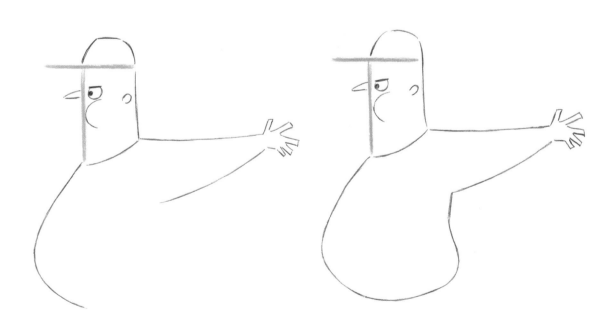

Sunglasses

Bright idea

"Marry me!"

Computer geek

The smallest princess

Future candy dish

Surf's up!

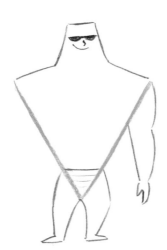

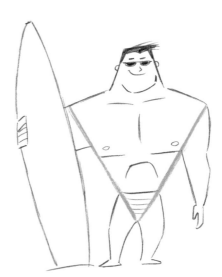

Big smile

Good-natured dad

"Hello, darling!"

Goofy grin

Proton power

Teacher's pet

Lovey dovey

Kiss ♥

College student

Friendly guy

"Anyone seen my horse?"

Bad mood dude

Sharp haircut

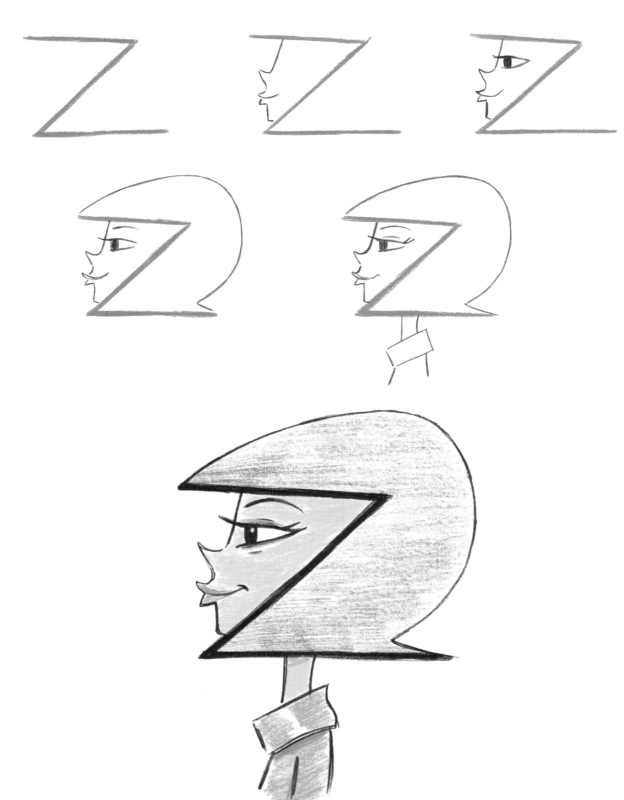

"Pleased to meet ya!"

Learn to Draw with Simple Shapes!

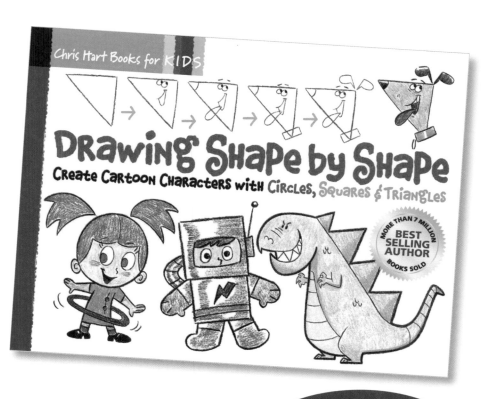

Connect with Chris on YouTube at **Youtube.com/user/chrishartbooks** and Facebook at **Facebook.com/CARTOONS.MANGA/**